e People Work

What Happens at a Vet's Office?

By Amy Hutchings

author/

pment

Gareth Stevens
PUBLISHING

Please visit our website, **www.garethstevens.com**.
For a free color catalog of all our high-quality books,
call toll free 1-800-542-2595 or fax 1-877-542-2596.

Library of Congress Cataloging-in-Publication Data

Hutchings, Amy.
     What happens at a vet's office? / by Amy Hutchings.
          p. cm. — Where people work)
     Includes bibliographical references.
     ISBN-10: 1-4339-0071-8 ISBN-13: 978-1-4339-0071-6 (lib. bdg.)
     ISBN-10: 1-4339-0135-8 ISBN-13: 978-1-4339-0135-5 (softcover)
     1. Veterinarians—Juvenile literature. 2. Veterinary medicine—Vocational guidance—
Juvenile literature. I. Title.
     SF756.H88   2009
     636.089—dc22
                                            2008027419

This edition first published in 2009 by
Gareth Stevens Publishing
111 East 14th Street, Suite 349
New York, NY 10003

Copyright © 2009 by Gareth Stevens, Inc.

Buddy® is a registered trademark of Gareth Steven, Inc. Used under license.

Executive Managing Editor: Lisa M. Herrington
Creative Director: Lisa Donovan
Designers: Alexandria Davis, Jennifer Ryder-Talbot
Photographer: Richard Hutchings
Publisher: Keith Garton

The publisher thanks Brett Levitzke, DVM, Medical Director of the Veterinary Emergency and
Referral Group in Brooklyn, New York, for his participation in the development of this book.

Printed in the United States of America

1 2 3 4 5 6 7 8 9 10 09 08

Hi, Kids!

I'm Buddy, your Gareth Stevens pal. Have you ever visited a vet's office? I'm here to show and tell what happens at a vet's office. So, come on. Turn the page and read along!

Animals go to the doctor, just as you do. A **vet** is a doctor who cares for animals. Jane's dog, Ginger, goes to the vet for a **checkup**.

First, a worker signs the family in at the desk. She takes their name and keeps track of Ginger's records.

Then they sit in the waiting room. The waiting room is filled with owners and their pets.

Now it is Ginger's turn! The vet's helper, called a **vet tech**, weighs Ginger on a **scale**.

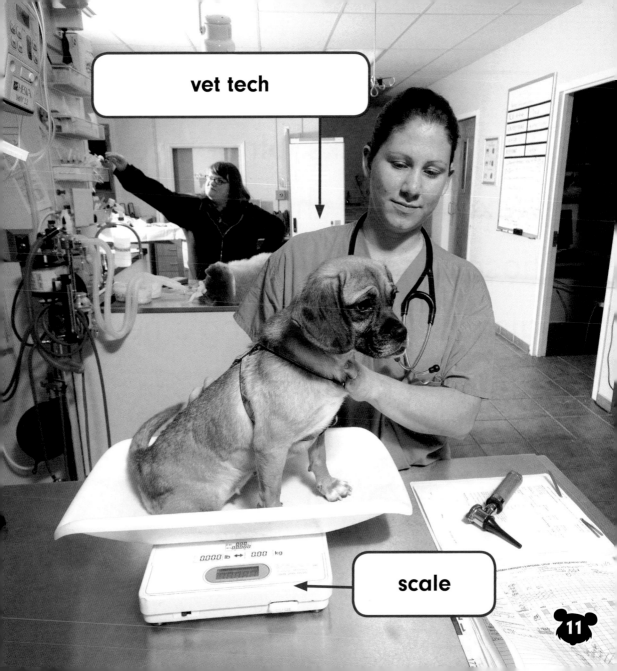

vet tech

scale

11

The vet checks Ginger's ears. Next, he will check her eyes, nose, and mouth. He will also listen to the dog's heart and feel her stomach.

vet

13

Ginger is a good **patient**. She gets a **shot** to keep her healthy.

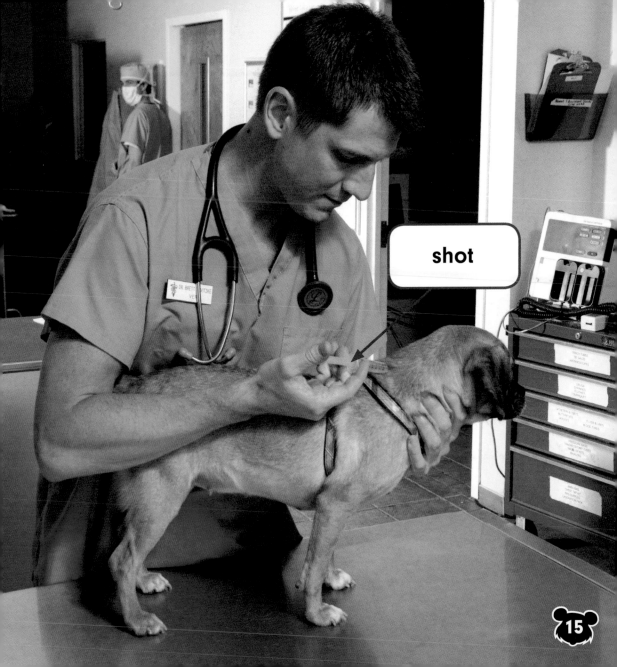

shot

15

The vet learns that Ginger stepped on a thorn. He checks the dog's paw.

Ginger gets an **X-ray** taken of her paw. A lab worker looks over the X-ray. Good news! Ginger's paw is fine.

X-ray

Ginger is healthy. The vet tells Jane how to care for Ginger. Jane gives Ginger a big hug!

🐻 Glossary

checkup: a medical exam to make sure a person or an animal is healthy

patient: a person or an animal who goes to the doctor or vet

scale: a machine that weighs things

shot: an injection of medicine

vet: an animal doctor (short for *veterinarian*)

vet tech: a trained worker who cares for animals and helps the vet

X-ray: a picture taken with a special camera used to see inside a body

For More Information

Books

Caring for Your Pets: A Book About Veterinarians.
Ann Owen (Coughlan Publishing, 2003)

Veterinarian. People in My Community (series).
JoAnn Early Macken (Gareth Stevens, 2003)

Web Sites

American Veterinary Medical Association (AVMA)

www.avma.org/careforanimals/animatedjourneys/
animatedfl.asp
Learn about pets and the people who care for them.

Petpourri from the AVMA

www.avma.org/careforanimals/kidscorner
Find fun activities to learn how to care for pets.

Publisher's note to educators and parents: Our editors have carefully reviewed these web sites to ensure that they are suitable for children. Many web sites change frequently, however, and we cannot guarantee that a site's future contents will continue to meet our high standards of quality and educational value. Be advised that children should be closely supervised whenever they access the Internet.

 # Index

About the Author

Amy Hutchings was part of the original production staff of *Sesame Street* for the first ten years of the show's history. She then went on to work with her husband, Richard, producing thousands of photographs for children's publishers. She has written several books, including *Firehouse Dog* and *Picking Apples and Pumpkins*. She lives in Rhinebeck, New York, along with many deer, squirrels, and wild turkeys.